FIX A CAR!

Chris Schweizer

:01

First Second
New York

Working on cars can be a great experience, but only if you do so **carefully**! Cars are heavy, complicated objects that have fast moving parts and dangerous chemicals, so always be diligent about safety!

Be sure to pay attention to the safety notes throughout the book. Read the packaging of any oils, fluids, or other products you use so you know how to handle them and dispose of them safely.

Follow instructions carefully when touching anything under the hood. Certain surfaces may be hot or corrosive.

Never allow an engine to run in a closed space (like a garage with the door shut). You can't see or smell the carbon monoxide in car exhaust, but it's deadly.

Cars have been known to fall off jacks. Never put your body, **or any part of your body**, under a car that is suspended on a jack.

Car repairs are easier and safer when you have an experienced helper. Make sure that an adult is on hand whenever you're doing repairs.

And when you go for a ride, **always** buckle your seat belt!

3

4

Which would defeat the purpose of Car Club!

The whole point of this endeavor is to help you learn how to take care of cars on your own.

But how are we supposed to take care of cars without any equipment?

You don't need a big, fancy garage like mine.

Most of the repairs and maintenance you'll be learning only require a few simple, affordable tools.

What you need in your own...

PORTABLE TOOL KIT for ON-THE-ROAD MAINTENANCE

SOCKET WRENCH SET

A **socket wrench** is a ratchet tool. It has different socket attachments that fit around bolts and nuts of different sizes.

It's a very handy tool because it only "works" in one direction at a time, so you can tighten a bolt by turning the handle one direction, then pull the handle back to where you started without loosening the bolt again. This means that you can keep working on one bolt without having to reposition your tool with each turn.

COMBINATION WRENCH SET

These **wrenches** are flat, making them essential for reaching into the many tight places in which nuts and bolts are nestled.

Since they're long, they give you more torque, which is the force that goes into a rotation. This means that they amplify the power of your turn.

PLIER SET

You'll need **pliers** to work on any of the electrical systems.

Make sure your set includes wire cutters and wire strippers!

BREAKER BAR

Sometimes bolts have been on too long or are just too tight to take off with a combination wrench or a socket wrench. A mechanic might use power tools, but with a little bit of effort, a **breaker bar** can get even the toughest bolt moving.

It's a lot like a socket wrench, but the longer handle offers a lot more torque, and the end is fixed (meaning it doesn't ratchet like a socket wrench). It still uses the same sockets, though!

SCREWDRIVERS

There are a lot of pieces in the car that require a **screwdriver** to take off (and put back!). You'll need Phillips and flathead types, both regular size and stubby for those tight places. You'll also want tiny ones for electronics work and a long flathead screwdriver that you can also use as a pry bar to separate parts that have gotten stuck together.

AUTOMOTIVE JACK

A **jack** lifts the car off the ground. Many cars come with jacks, so there's a good chance that you might already have one folded up under the back seat or under a panel in the trunk.

You'll need a jack to change a tire, but if you want to do more than that, you'll need to get **jack stands,** too. Working on a car being held up by just a jack can be **very** unsafe, and the only time you should do it is when changing a tire.

You'll also want...

ELECTRICAL TAPE

...for emergency repairs on wires and hoses!

A HEADLAMP & A FLASHLIGHT

...to see into a dark engine and underneath the car!

GLOVES

...to protect your hands!

Some of the work you'll be doing might require other tools, but those give you a great start.

You can keep them in your car for emergency repairs. Except for the breaker bar and the jack, they'll all fit in a tackle box, toolbox, or small laundry bin.

But you know what? You'll have a lot **fewer** emergency repairs **if** you pay attention to our **first lesson**.

What's the first lesson?

THE FIRST LESSON: PREVENTIVE MAINTENANCE

If you check your car's systems regularly, you can catch little problems before they become big ones!

That's what we'll be doing today.

Catching little problems?

Maybe!

We're going to learn about what the different systems do.

Once we understand **that**, it's easy to make sure that they're doing what they're supposed to!

So let's start with **fluids**.

Fluids are the easiest part of your car to check.

Mason, could you pop your hood for me?

There are **six** fluids that you can check in most cars.

But there are only **four** here.

Oil, **washer fluid**, **brake fluid**, and **coolant**.

Brake fluid

Oil fill cap

Windshield washer fluid

Oil level dipstick

Engine coolant

The other two are **transmission fluid** and **power steering fluid**.

This is a newer model car. Many new cars have electric power steering and don't have an easy way to check the transmission fluid the way you can in older cars.

Don't worry, we'll look at **those** in **Abner's** car.

Oh yeah!

11

The first thing you ought to do is check the oil.

Your car engine has lots of moving parts, and almost all of these parts are made of **metal**.

Some parts move **thousands** of times **every minute.** If they were to grind against each other, these parts would wear out very quickly!

To keep the parts from wearing out (and to keep them cool and clean), they are coated in an ever-moving film of motor oil, which works as a lubricant.

3. The **oil pump** uses pressure to force the oil through the **filter** and into the engine.

This is the oil pump.

This is the oil pan.

4. The clean oil flows through lots of **channels** in the engine to coat the different moving parts.

1. The oil sits in the **oil pan**.

2. It's pulled up through the **sump strainer**.

5. The oil travels through a return channel back to the oil pan to repeat its journey.

This is the oil filter.

The engine is very hot, so the oil that goes through it eventually gets cooked away.

And if your engine is older, it will burn through oil faster than a new one.

Checking your oil level is easy. You just look for the **dipstick**.

The dipstick is a long, flat piece of metal that ends in a ring.

Every type of car is different, so if you have trouble finding your dipstick, check the owner's manual.

If you don't have a manual in your glove compartment, you can usually find it online.

Using the ring, pull the dipstick from its tube.

Wipe the oil off the dipstick with a rag or a paper towel.

Once you've wiped it clean, insert the dipstick **all the way** back into its tube.

Then you pull it out again.

Man, this is like the Hokey Pokey.

"You put the dipstick in, you take the dipstick out, you put the dipstick in, and you shake it all about..."

You better **not** shake it all about.

You splatter oil on my jacket, I'm gonna bring the thunder.

15

To make sure you have enough coolant, check the reservoir.

It's made of hard plastic, so it's pretty sturdy, but be careful when working around it. Plastic is easy to crack.

Never open the reservoir cap unless your car has had time to cool. Otherwise you could be hit in the face with scalding, toxic steam. Nobody wants that!

CAUTION CAUTION COOLANT Philips

The reservoir should have markings that will let you know if it's low.

The coolant that you use is called **antifreeze**. It has a higher boiling point and a lower freezing point than water, so it will keep your car running smoothly even in very cold or very hot weather.

ANTI-FREEZE

Pure antifreeze doesn't transfer heat as well as antifreeze mixed fifty-fifty with water does.

Some antifreeze comes premixed. **Be sure to read the label** to know whether or not to add water!

When you **do** need to add antifreeze, you add it to the reservoir. Be sure to use a funnel when pouring!

Funnels are for chumps!

My hands are **crazy** steady.

Years of gaming.

I don't **need** a funnel to make a clean pour.

Well, antifreeze is **very** poisonous. It's also very **sweet**.

If some gets on the ground, it might attract dogs, who will lap it up.

My hands are steady, too, but I wouldn't bet a pet's life on it.

Funnels are **all right**.

18

The final two fluids we'll be checking aren't accessible on Mason's car, so we'll take a look at Abner's, which is a little older.

I prefer "classic."

Your car's power steering fluid can be found in the power steering fluid reservoir.

Check the manual to see where it is?

Power steering uses hydraulic fluid to amplify the force the driver uses to turn the wheel. When the **steering wheel** is turned, pressure from the hydraulics helps to push the **rack** connected to the **wheels**, turning them without much physical effort from the driver.

steering wheel

The **rotary valve** recognizes that the steering wheel is turning and opens a channel for the power steering fluid.

Many power steering fluid reservoirs have a small dipstick built into the cap.*

Wipe it, reinsert it, and check the level!

Fluid lines transport the pressurized fluid into a cylinder, pushing a piston attached to the rack and allowing the rack to turn the tires with ease.

The **steering column** controls the **pinion**, a small gear that moves the rack.

The **pump**, powered by an engine belt, provides the pressure for the fluid, but it runs constantly. So to use less energy, many manufacturers are switching to electric power steering, which uses no fluid.

The **rack** is the companion gear to the pinion, a straight series of gear teeth that moves left and right to make the **tie-rods** push or pull the **tires**, causing the car to turn.

* Many other reservoirs are made of partially clear plastic so that you can see the fluid level just by looking at them!

Next, we'll check the **transmission fluid**.

THE TRANSMISSION

is a series of gears designed to use the engine's energy as efficiently as possible.

Large gears take longer to go around. This means the engine's energy turns into **power**, helping a heavy car to start moving, pull something, or climb a steep hill.

As gears get smaller, the energy created by the engine allows for the wheels to turn faster. There is less power but more speed.

As the car gains momentum, it requires less power to move, so the gears become smaller to allow the engine's energy to be used almost exclusively for **speed**.

Some cars change gears automatically. This is **automatic transmission**.

Others require the driver to use a clutch and change the gears manually with a stick shift. this is **manual transmission**.

1st Gear

2nd Gear

3rd Gear

4th Gear

5th Gear

Each successive gear gets a little smaller in diameter (offset by its increasingly larger partner gear below) so that the car can go faster when in higher gears.

The transmission fluid **lubricates** these gears and the parts that shift them, as well as helping to protect them from wear and to keep them cool.

You check its level with a dipstick the same way you would the oil. You can check your manual to find its location in the engine, but it's usually easy to spot.

Your oil dipstick ends in a ring, but your transmission dipstick?

It might have a flat grip.

Your car needs to be cool to check **most** of your fluids, but your transmission fluid level reads best when the engine is warmed up and running.

(Some transmission dipsticks have a "cold" and "hot" read marking, allowing you to check the fluid level when it's not running, too.)

or

Front

Back

HOT

COLD

Abner, turn your car on and let it run for a minute.

You got it, Ms. Gritt!

VRMM

So why can't you check the transmission level on **my** car?

Car manufacturers argue that only **professionals** should mess around with the transmission system.

Transmission fluid will easily last throughout most warranty periods, so making it difficult or impossible for the driver to add to it saves the manufacturer money.

Most new cars use transmission fluid created specifically for that engine. If a customer or shop puts in another fluid, it might damage the transmission, and if the car is still under warranty, then the manufacturer has to cover the expensive repair costs.

But what happens **after** that warranty period? The transmission fluid will need to be changed eventually, right?

Yes, but **you** won't be able to easily diagnose whether or not your car's transmission fluid needs changing. You'll need to rely on a trusted mechanic.

Let's check yours, Abner.

Wipe the dipstick* and reinsert it to get a read.

Even if your transmission fluid is at the "full" mark, check its color. If it's kind of red, you're good; if it looks burnt or brown or black, it's probably time to change it.

Still good

Change

*Paper towels can shed lint and dust, and these can contaminate your car's oil. Use a cloth!

Keeping an eye on your car is **important**.

When your car is running smoothly, it's easy to forget about maintaining it.

But by the time your car starts to **show** problems, it's usually **after** the problem has become bad enough to affect a system.

Those problems can be very expensive and time-consuming to fix. But if you're **vigilant** about your car's upkeep, you can avoid many of those problems altogether!

This doesn't mean that you have to check the fluids every time that you get in the car! If you're not experiencing problems driving, you can check most of them just a couple of times a year.

I recommend when summer starts and when winter starts.

The exception is your **motor oil**. Since your car burns away the oil, it gets used up more quickly than the other fluids.

If you want to really stay on top of things, checking your oil level every couple of weeks is a good plan.

So as long as we keep an eye on our fluid levels, we should be able to avoid most preventable problems with our engine?

It'll help, but keeping your fluids in good order is only **one** part of preventive maintenance.

You also want to make sure that the engine itself is up to snuff.

You should examine the more fragile parts of your engine once a month (and before any long trip).

Taking a few minutes to give your engine a good once-over will help you keep your car running well for a long, long time.

Let's start with the **battery**!

BATTERY

Inside your engine are cylinders in which your car's fuel is burned, becoming the energy that moves your car. That same energy keeps the pistons in those cylinders pumping, burning more fuel. But where does the energy come from that gets those pistons pumping in the first place?

It comes from the **battery**!

Positive terminal (red)

Negative terminal (black)

(or occasionally blue!)

The battery's number one job is to start the engine. Once the engine has started, it uses the fuel to supply the power necessary to move the car.* The engine then uses the alternator to recharge the battery as it runs, preparing it for the next time it has to start the car.

There are a lot of places where your battery can show wear and tear.

❋ HYBRID & ELECTRIC VEHICLES

Hybrid cars use a battery to power the car itself, **teaming up** with the engine's fuel to help the car run as efficiently as possible.

When the car first accelerates or drives at low speeds, the **battery** powers the car. As it speeds up, the **fuel** provides the power!

And just like a standard car battery, it is recharged by the engine itself when the fuel begins to power that engine.

Electric cars are powered **entirely** by batteries. Those batteries can be recharged by plugging them into an electric power supply.

Your car's battery is filled with **sulfuric acid**, and sometimes that acid and its vapors leak out, creating powdery deposits around the the battery's terminal.

Deposits

Left unchecked, these deposits can grow rapidly, causing the contact between the battery and the electrical system to fail.

Really bad deposits

These deposits are easy to clean away. But they're very toxic! You don't want to get them on your skin, and you definitely don't want to inhale them or get them in your eyes.

Wear gloves and safety goggles!

And don't wipe your hands on your clothes if you don't want to stain them forever.

Before you try to clean a crusty battery, it's important to disconnect it so that you don't accidentally shock yourself or the car's computer or electrical systems. We disconnect the battery by removing **both** of its cables.

Make sure to remove the grounded* cable first!

Both cables are needed to complete the electrical circuit. Without the positive cable, the open circuit will try to close itself. Since the negative cable is grounded to the car, that makes the whole car a part of the open circuit. Accidentally touch the car or battery with a tool, and you could create sparks, or even...

...a violent, acid-spewing EXPLOSION!

*If your car is less than fifty years old, the grounded cable will be the negative cable.

You also want to check your **drive belts**.

The belts bring power from the engine's crankshaft to other essential parts, like the water pump, the power steering pump, and the alternator.

Some cars use individual belts called **V-belts** to power these systems.

Others use a single winding belt called a **serpentine belt**.

These belts are made of rubber, and they can decay and crack over time. A cracked belt can break while you're driving, leaving your engine unable to function.

It's also a good idea to check your tires.

Do any of you know the **penny test**?

I do!

Yeah, me, too.

Your tire treads wear away over time. If your treads are too low, your tire could blow out.

You're going 70 when that happens?

SCREEE KERASH!

Not necessarily. You still ought to check your treads, though.*

You take a **penny**, turn it upside down, and stick it into the shallowest part of the tread.

If the hair on the top of Honest Abe's head is visible, consider getting new tires. If not, your treads are good.

Good tread!

That's it exactly, Esther!

But if you can't find a penny, you can get a **tread depth gauge** for pretty cheap at a tire or auto parts store.

*Make sure your tires are at their proper pressure to ensure that a tread test is accurate! We'll check tire pressure on page 68.

Also look on the sides for bulges or gouges that can come from scraping curbs.

Between checking your fluid levels and giving your car a quick visual inspection like this every couple of weeks, you can **catch** problems before they **become** problems!

SLAM

We've just got one last thing to check.

My rims?

My tint?

Spoiler? Speakers? My ride's got a **lot** to check, Ms. Gritt.

Windshield wipers!

Oh.

And yours need to be changed, Abner.

See how the end is split and separated? That and the rubber becoming brittle with age will keep your wiper blades from clearing away water properly.

Your windshield wiper blades usually need to be changed once or twice a year.

Changing Abner's will be our **first project**!

I've got some spare blades in the garage!

Me, **I** was kind of hoping we'd do **racing stripes**.

CHANGING YOUR WINDSHIELD WIPER BLADES

Make sure you know what size wiper blades to use. Your manual will tell you, or you can measure your old blades yourself!

It's not uncommon for the driver and passenger side blades to be two different sizes, so checking **is** important.

When you have your new blades, pull the old wipers away from the windshield.

Most will stay out on their own, but if yours won't, fold a towel and put it underneath the old blade so that the spring-mounted arm won't scratch or chip the windshield when you detach the blade.

Different cars use different mechanisms to attach the blades to the wiper arms.

Each of these mechanisms operates differently, so look for buttons or levers to press or pull to disconnect your blade.

When you've released the catch, pull the old blade out. You might have to wiggle it a little if it's been on for a while!

Slide the new wiper in and make sure that it clicks into place.

Once you gently lay the wiper back against the windshield, you repeat the process with the other wiper.

29

What do you mean, "get out of it"?

If Ms. Gritt isn't your teacher, then Car Club doesn't give you extra credit for physics.

And you're not fixing a car or anything.

Not being old enough to drive doesn't mean you can't fix cars.

Yeah, we just **like cars**. We like knowing how they work and how to take care of them and how to fix stuff.

I get that.

Me, I don't know squat about how trucks **work**, but I **love** driving. Figure if I'm going to be serious about it, I ought to know at least a little about **what** I'm driving.

It **is** a nice truck. What's it got, a 6.0?

Couldn't tell you, Rocky.

That's why I'm **here!**

Hi, Lena. Go ahead and pull all the way up to the garage, all right?

So what are we doing today, Ms. Gritt?

Today?

Today we're going to **change our oil**!

And we're going to do it...

...on Lena's truck.

Why Lena's?

I mean, you're fronting the costs for the supplies for these lessons, and we really appreciate that, Ms. G. But I'm just curious as to whether you've got a rotation in mind or something.

My car, Lena's truck, Mason's car, repeat?

That's a fair way to go about it, sure.

But there's a more **practical** reason for using Lena's truck for our oil change.

The truck is **lifted**.

That means it has been raised up higher than when it was manufactured.

I like to go mudding.

When a car or truck has been lifted, it gives the driver the option to add larger tires that raise the vehicle.

This truck has been lifted by adding extra **leaves**. A leaf is a flat type of spring.

The truck is high enough off the ground that we can comfortably get underneath it.

An oil change requires getting underneath the vehicle, so Lena's will be easiest.

This one's tricky. It's got a splash shield, which protects the engine from road debris but makes underside access trickier.

Some car maintenance might require removing the shield, but you can get to the oil pan and filter by going around its side.

Make sure you've got your gloves on and that you've got your drain pan or bucket ready to catch the old oil.

There is a plug on the oil pan, and you'll remove it to drain the oil.

Using the closed end of your combination wrench, loosen the plug and be ready for the oil to first leak, then shoot out.

Keep turning until the plug comes off. Keep your hands clear in case some of the oil is still hot!

Now we give it a few minutes to drain.

Different engines require different amounts of oil. Lena's takes six quarts.

"Check the manual."

If you're worried that you have an oil leak, now's the time to look under your car for **drips!***

When you've finished pouring in the new oil, close up the cap.

You're almost done!

"Almost"?

We've still got to clean up the oil.

I did a report on it for Earth Day, back in ninth grade.

You can't just throw it away, and you need to be careful not to spill it.

Used oil has toxic chemicals in it, plus bits of metal. Oil doesn't dissolve in water, so when it rains or when it's hosed away, it ends up getting washed into sewers and drains or into yards or ditches.

It can poison plants and animals, contaminate drinking water, and mess up water treatment plants.

That's right, Abner. So we pour the used oil from the drain tray into something that we can seal...

old auto fluid bottles are good...

and we take it somewhere to be recycled.

*To avoid leaks, tighten the oil pan bolts and replace leak-prone parts like rubber gaskets and seals. You can also use **stop leak** oil additives, which soften rubber and plug leaks.

Look online to find your nearest oil recycling location.

It might be a city or county hazardous waste disposal site, or it might be a nearby auto parts store.

Don't forget to take the old oil filter with the oil!

All right! Now you know how to change your own oil.

Now, you need to be able to decide whether or not it's worthwhile to do so.

What do you mean?

Because you're not paying for the cost of labor, a lot of car maintenance and repair will cost less if you do it yourself.

Oil changes are the **exception**.

When I was young, it saved you a good deal of money to change your own oil, but oil changes have gotten much cheaper over the years.

Depending on the type of oil your engine uses, you might save a lot, but you may only save a dollar or two. If you factor in the cost of a filter wrench and drain pan, it might cost you **more** money to change it yourself!

It's always good to know how to do things yourself, and changing your own oil can be fun, especially if you like working on cars.

But if you're doing it to save money, be sure to add up your costs and compare!

Now, use the hose to wash off any oil that's on your skin. It's toxic, remember!

And Mason, I noticed your car has been **squeaking**, so we'll all look into that **next** week!

All right, class...

Dis- missed!

Thank you, sir!

Mason, hold back a sec.

What's up, Teach?

I noticed that you signed up for testing next week.

Yes, sir. Keen on getting that red belt.

*See page 26 for a refresher on drive belts.

That might just mean that you need to adjust the tensioner using a socket wrench (or maybe a breaker bar, since it will be tight), but you might need to replace the tensioner altogether.

The tensioner nut makes the belt tension looser or tighter.

If the noise **doesn't change** when you spray the belt with water, then it's not the belt squeaking but a **pulley**.

The most likely cause of a pulley squeak is that a bearing has gone bad inside the pulley.

If that's happened, you can remove the old pulley and replace it with one from an auto parts store.

But don't think that your bearings are just fine because the squeak changes when you spray the belt!

They could **still** be responsible for the squeaking noise.

This squeak **disappeared** when you sprayed the belt.

It did! But it'll come back. If the squeaking stops when wetted, that means that it's either a problem with the belt itself or with the belt's alignment.

Sorry...

"Alignment"?

Alignment is when a straight line is created when you go from the position of one thing to the position of another.

Your belt goes through a lot of points, and each point has to align with all the others.

If one of those points isn't exactly where it should be, the belt will be **misaligned**. This will put extra pressure on the pulleys and will cause wear to the belt.

What could make a pulley move out of place?

There could be a couple of different causes for that, Esther.

What I want you to do is sketch a little diagram of where the serpentine belt goes.

We'll want to look at it when we put the belt back.

Oh, sure, I can do **that**.

You **could** just snap a photo if you've got a phone with a camera, but I love a good diagram!

So the tensioner? We're going to use our breaker bar to release the tension that it's putting on the belt.

Do you know which way to turn the nut?

You turn stuff left—counterclockwise—to loosen it, right?

Righty tighty, lefty loosey.

Usually, that's correct. But the reason I bring it up now is that sometimes the threads on **tensioners** are **reversed**.

Any guesses on how to find out which way this car's tensioner threads need to be turned?

"Check the manual."

Goodness. Y'all **are** learning!

It doesn't say anything one way or the other.

That usually means that it's the standard counterclockwise-to-loosen threading.

Still, it doesn't hurt to do a quick online search for your car's year and model, and "tensioner thread direction."

Looks like it's regular. Lefty loosey.

Great! On a newer car like this, you can call a dealership, and they can probably tell you, too.

How goes the diagram, Rocky?

That's the **idler pulley**.

So it connects to the idler? What does the idler do?

There isn't an "idler."

It's called an idler pulley because it doesn't directly supply power to a part of the engine like the other pulleys do.

If it doesn't serve a purpose, why is it there at all?

It doesn't power a part, but it **does** serve a purpose.

It supplies tension to the belt and helps to define the belt's path, moving it out of the way of other engine parts.

This one's only got one bolt. Lena, why don't you remove it?

Okay.

Wait, we're taking it off without a new pulley to put in its place?

Figured it was probably a pulley, so I grabbed one of each for this model from Otto. He said I could just bring back the unused ones later, and pay for the one we kept.

Got the bolt off, Ms. Gritt.

Thanks, Lena! Now we can slip the pulley off...

...and check to see if its bearing really has gone bad!

If we pull the bolt out, we can spin it on our finger, giving it a listen.

Sounds kind of scrapey.

And see how it looks a little worn on the edges? This is our culprit, all right.

Let's check the new pulley against the old one, make sure that they're the same size...

...and if it looks right, then we slide the bolt back in and screw the washer onto the back.

Lena, think you can put it on like you took it off?

You got it!

Once it's on nice and tight, give it a spin.

Smooth as a greasy baby!

Eww.

Okay, Mason, you can put the belt back in place before we tighten the tensioner again.

Use Rocky's diagram to make sure it goes through the pulleys the correct way, and be sure it's centered on each pulley!

That'll wrap up today's lesson, I think. Anybody have something specific that they'd like to learn next Saturday?

Ooh!

Ooh!

52

53

It's raining pretty hard, Abner.

We can't do anything to the car's exterior in this downpour, and if we tried to work on the inside, it would get **soaked**!

There was only a thirty percent chance of rain today, which is why I didn't cancel Car Club...

...but it doesn't look like it's going to let up, and we really oughtn't work in rain this heavy unless an emergency gives us no other choice.

Should somebody call Mason? Tell him we're calling it quits today?

Naw. Here he comes.

He's going a little fast for this weather.

The roads are slick. You shouldn't have been driving so fast!

You're the one who was giving me grief last time about being late! I was going the speed limit.

Yeah, while taking a corner in heavy rain. What if a **kid** had run out in front of you?

You're like the least responsible driver I know, Abner. I've seen you try to steer with your **feet**.

In an empty parking lot, **not** speeding through a **neighborhood**.

I wasn't speeding!

Gentlemen!

Mason, whether or not you were obeying the speed limit, you **were** going too fast for the road conditions today.

Sorry, Ms. Gritt. I was running a little late, and I kept getting behind slow cars and hitting traffic lights.

We'll get to your tire in a few minutes, Mason.

Let's give our umbrella muscles a rest for the moment, up on the porch.

When you're in a hurry, you're putting yourself in a position to make bad decisions.

You'll take more risks, because every second that you shave off your trip seems to matter.

Your fellow drivers are part of a **community** of folks whose adherence to the rules and courtesies of the road helps to keep one another safe, but when you're in a **hurry**, they're not your neighbors of the road.

They're **obstacles**.

When you view your fellow drivers through that lens, it makes it easy to ignore that courtesy that helps the roads run smoothly.

And when you drive in a way that other drivers don't expect, the chances for an accident increase dramatically.

Not to mention that when you're sour from your drive, you're likely to **stay** sour when you get to where you're going.

It can be hard to make yourself leave with plenty of time to reach your destination.

Everyone's busy. Everyone's in the middle of something when they know they have to get moving.

But it's **important**. Just as important to the safety of you and your car as brake fluid or working seat belts.

If you know you're going to be late, call whoever you're meeting and let them know. Then drive like you have time.

But that's for occasions when lateness **can't be helped**, and if we're honest with ourselves, we know that most of the time, it can be if we choose to stop what we're doing in order to leave with plenty of time in our pocket.

Being late is like running out of gas. Yeah, it'll happen sometimes, but it shouldn't happen often, and it won't when we're diligent.

I've got a lot on my plate right now, Ms. Gritt.

It's tough to get from one thing to another on time.

I know, Mason. And I know that you're expected to put in the full time at all of your activities.

But talk to whoever's coordinating them. Let them know if you have to leave a few minutes early or arrive a few minutes late.

If none of them are flexible, then you might need to think about which activities are the highest priority and putting the others on hold for the immediate future.

But all of them are important!

I get you.

It's like my class tracks for next year. I can either go the math and science track, or I can go the humanities track.

But that's **hooey**. I like trig and geometry **and** reading and writing stories.

Having to pick one thing over the other is like abandoning half of myself, you know?

Yeah.

Mason's working crazy hard to keep up with baseball, and his classes, and his Eagle Scout project, and who knows what else, right?

A lot.

A lot else.

I'm not giving up writing just because I want to do higher-level math.

Mason shouldn't have to choose between the things **he's** trying to accomplish.

59

How did you know you had a spare tire but not know where it was?

I forgot. I've never used it.

Your parking brake is on. Good! That's important.

First thing we're going to do is wedge the wheels so that there's no chance of the car rolling off the jack.

I've never seen anybody do any wheel-wedging when changing a tire.

Most people don't bother, but if you've got the means to do it, you might as well.

Even if you keep yourself safely clear of the vehicle while you're changing the tire...

which you **should**...

your car could be badly damaged if it rolled off the jack. Why take the risk?

A pair of wedges, also called wheel chocks, will only run you a few dollars. They're worth keeping with your jack!

If you don't have wedges, use a couple of rocks.

If your back tire is flat, put them against your front tires. If your front tire is flat, put them against the back tires.

And the piece of wood?

Put it under the jack. The vehicle puts a lot of weight on the jack, and if the asphalt is chipped or uneven, then the jack could shift when it settles.

If there's wood underneath, then the jack will dig into the **wood** as it settles, keeping your car sturdy while it's lifted.

But before we use the jack, we're going to loosen the **lug nuts**!

Once it's close, make sure it's squarely on the wood, and line up the top exactly where you want it to make contact.

Now raise the jack until the flat tire comfortably clears the ground.

Now you can remove the lug nuts.

You should be able to unscrew most of them by hand, but the last one will have pressure on it from supporting the entire wheel all by itself, so you'll probably need to use the tire iron.

Carefully pull the tire straight toward you until it's off its lug bolts.

Be gentle so as not to rock the car off the jack.

Set it on its side, so that it doesn't roll away.

Got your spare ready?

I've got it ready.

This is a compact, limited-use tire. Folks call them "donuts."

Donuts serve one purpose: to get you to a place where you can repair your tire or buy a new one.

They're not meant to go fast or far, and many of your car's systems don't work properly with them, so **never** just drive around on a donut.

If you can afford to do so, it's a **really** good idea to replace your donut tire with a **full-size spare**.

You can get the exact same kind of wheel and tire as what your car is already using and store that in the spare tire well.

If the well is made for a donut, there's a chance a full-size tire won't fit, so check.

And if you find yourself getting new tires, that's the perfect opportunity to land a full-size spare.

Just keep whichever of your old tires is in the best shape, and have it mounted on a new spare wheel!

Having a full-size spare is important if you ever take long trips. If you have a full size, you can change your tire and finish your trip, repairing the flat tire when you get back home.

If not, your trip will have to be put on hold while you try to find an open tire repair place and wait to get the flat tire fixed or replaced.

Is the spare on nice and solid?

As solid as it can be without putting the lug nuts back on, I guess.

Well, let's put them back on! To distribute the weight evenly, put each new bolt on across from the last one.

Tighten them with your fingers. Don't use the tire iron yet since it could rock the car.

Once they're all on reasonably snug, lower the jack. With a bottle jack, that means turning the handle again, counterclockwise this time.

Let it go down until the wheel is resting on the ground, but don't take it farther than that. The weight of the car should still be on the jack rather than the tire.

Now that it can't fall off the jack, go ahead and use that tire iron to tighten those lug nuts. Tight as you can, Mason!

That's as tight as I can do it.

Great! Now we lower the jack the rest of the way, and put the flat tire in the spare tire well. Put the jack away, too, and the tire iron.

You can use a tire gauge (a small, cheap tool you should keep in your car) to check the pressure on the spare. Make sure it hasn't lost air while waiting to be used.

It'll say how many pounds of pressure per square inch the tire should be inflated to on the tire itself.

This says "60 PSI."

To check your tire's pressure, unscrew the little air cap and put the open side of the tire gauge tightly against the valve.

The air inside the tire will push a little reader out of the bottom of the tire gauge.

Check that against your tire's specifications, and if it's low, find an air pump at a gas station and fill the tire, checking your gauge as you do so.

Mason, that tire likely isn't repairable. You'll need to get a new one, first thing.

≶sigh≷
I know.

All right, youngsters. Time to get out of the rain. And if it's sunny next Saturday...

Keep at it until no more dust comes off. It may take just a couple of whacks; it may take a couple dozen!

Now, you can't beat the floors themselves, but you can give them a good vacuuming with the shop vac.

Get all around the pedals, and under and between the seats!

If there are stains, spray them with the carpet shampoo. Read the bottle to know how long it should sit.

You don't have to get car-specific shampoo; any carpet shampoo will do.

While your shampoo sits, we'll start cleaning all the nooks and crannies. Now's when you want your brushes!

First, we'll use a little vent-cleaning brush. You can slide one of these in and out of your air vents.

(or you could use a cotton swab)

You can use an old tooth-brush to clean inside cracks and crannies, like the inside of a door handle or next to the gearshift.

Use that canned air to blast dust out of console buttons and any cracks or crevices that the brushes can't reach.

Once you've gotten all the spots where dirt and crumbs can hide, you can wipe and scrub away all the debris you kicked up.

Spray or pour a little bit of your multipurpose cleaner onto a rag...

...then use it to clean the dashboard, the steering wheel, the steering column, the console, all that stuff.

Yep! But the outside isn't the **only** part of the windows that needs to be cleaned.

Residue given off by plastic and the grease from your skin and hair can build up on the glass, and that gives dust and grime a foothold.

This can make parts of your windshield and windows murkier than others. You may not notice in daylight...

But at night, it can produce **glares** from the headlights and taillights of other cars.

This can make it harder to determine where those other cars are, if there are obstacles in the road, and even where the road itself is. Poor visibility can lead to bad accidents!

Now, regular glass cleaner is fine for most windows and windshields, **unless** they have custom tinting, like Abner's.

Hmm.

Many glass cleaners are ammonia based. The ammonia can break down the tint and cause it to bubble and peel over time.

You can get tint-specific window cleaners at an auto parts store, or you can cut your window cleaner with water, mixing a solution that is about one-fourth cleaner with the rest being water.

If you want to be really crafty and avoid the ammonia altogether, you can make up your own solution with water and a few capfuls each of rubbing alcohol and white vinegar.

Whatever you're using to clean, you won't have to use much to do the job!

When you're cleaning your windows, your best bet is a microfiber cloth.

These cloths have much, much tinier fibers, which means that they can pick up much tinier particles, which the larger fibers of regular cloth might brush right past.

Since much of the residue that builds up on your windows is tiny and slick, microfibers can do a better job than any old rag.

Because the small fibers do a lot of the work themselves, you don't need nearly as much cleaning solution to break down the grime to where the cloth can clear it away.

Just spray a little bit on the cloth itself every few wipes. That way you don't end up overspraying the glass and having to clean up drips.

Do we clean outsides of the windows next?

Nope. We do all the inside before any outside.

Our last step on the inside is to polish the parts that aren't cloth, like the dashboard, the steering wheel, and the seats if they're made of vinyl or leather.

Some people like to use an oil-based protectant on their interiors. These can protect the car's interior to a degree and can make them look rich and shiny if you reapply it regularly.

Shiny!

But oil-based products aren't great for vinyl and plastic, and I don't like the greasiness that sometimes accompanies it.

Doesn't bother me any! Can I have some of that protectant for my dash, Ms. G?

I don't have any here, Abner, but you can pick up a bottle anywhere that sells car stuff.

Also, keep in mind that if your car has leather seats or interior parts, you should apply a leather conditioner after cleaning it.

Otherwise that leather will eventually start to crack!

Once the insides of everyone's cars are clean, we'll move to the outsides.

Make sure that your mats are back inside and vacuumed and that your windows and doors are shut.

WASHING YOUR CAR

SOME TIPS TO KEEP IN MIND

Be prepared to get wet. Don't wear a tuxedo or something, unless you're, like, doing a bit.

Incongruity is **funny**, baby.

Make sure that your car is parked in the shade or that it's a cloudy day. You want to be the one doing the drying. Don't let the sun beat you to it.

Have all your tools on hand and ready to go. You'll need some cloths or towels, a sponge or a washing mitt, a scrub brush, car washing detergent, and a couple of buckets.

Start with the tires. Use a hose to spray away as much dirt, mud, gravel, and grime that may have accumulated on the tires and in the wheel wells.

RAGS

Before you do any scrubbing, give your whole car a once-over with the hose, and if you see any dirt or bird poop, use the spray to get as much of it off as you can.

Bird poop contains uric acid, which will eat through paint.

Deicing chemicals and road salt, used to keep streets safe and clear in the winter, can cause cars to rust rapidly.

Dead bugs on the front of your car are acidic, too.

Now get your buckets full of water.*

One of them should be **just** water...

...and the other should have a little bit of **car-washing detergent** mixed in as you fill it.

Make sure the detergent that you're using is made for cars. Regular soap and cleaning detergent can strip away the wax and clear finish on a car, which will in turn hurt the paint.

Once your buckets are full and the loose dirt has been sprayed clean from the car, focus on the **tires**.

The tires are probably the dirtiest part of your vehicle, and they can pick up bits of grit that can scratch your car if they get on your cleaning rags. Getting all that stuff out of the picture before working on the car's body is the best way to go.

Take a rag and, if needed, a firm-bristled brush, dip them in the detergent water, and get whatever might still be on the tires.

You'll empty and clean the bucket and mix up another batch of detergent water when you're done with the tires. The old water's too dirty!

Get inside all the holes or spokes of your wheels and around the bolts!

Do this for all four wheels, then give it another spray with the hose to clear off any grit that might be left.

*Warm water works best if it's available.

Why not let it air-dry? We're in the shade. Wouldn't it be easier on the car?

It'll leave little water spots. They'll make the car look dirtier, but they can also eat away at the finish and maybe cause the car to rust.

Go over it all lightly with a dry towel. If your towel gets damp, switch to another towel!

When your car is nice and dry, it's a good idea to wax it. Putting **wax** on your car protects it from harsh sunlight, rain, and the road dirt and bugs that pepper it during a drive.

Wax comes in paste, liquid, or spray!

WAX

WAX

CARNAUBA WAX

Think of it as a little bit of armor between the elements and the surface of your vehicle.

Wax

Use less than you think you'll need, putting about a quarter-sized bit on the cloth or foam applicator that comes with the wax.

WAX

Too much will make your finish look uneven and gunky, and it'll be harder to remove!

Do small sections at a time and rub the wax onto the surface of the car in small, light circles, leaving an even coat.

The wax container will tell you how long to leave the wax, but you should check for yourself.

Drag your finger across the car's surface.

If it smudges, you need to wait.

If it's clear, it's time to wipe the wax away.

ADDING A RACING STRIPE

*Wax protects your car from dirt, grime... and paint! Never paint over a coat of wax, it won't take.

My **goodness**, Lena!

You certainly had an adventure.

Yes, ma'am.

I was wondering... did you have anything specific you were wanting to cover today?

Oh no!

She's gonna try to rope us in to washing her truck again!

That's **not** why I'm asking.

When I cleaned the mud off my lights, I realized that one of my **taillights** was out.

I bought a replacement at Otto's but figured we could put it in together.

I think that's a fine idea, Lena. And it'll give us a chance to talk about a car's electrical system.

Understanding your car's

ELECTRICAL SYSTEM

Your battery gives power to the starter to get the engine going.

The engine cranks the alternator, which recharges the battery.

Receiving a steady charge from the alternator, the battery supplies power to the car's electrical components.

The current passes through a voltage regulator to keep it at a steady level.

Plenty of stuff in your car is powered by the electrical system.

Windshield wipers

Radio and speakers

Satellite connection for GPS or streaming

Defroster

Power windows and power locks

Plus, it's what you use to car-charge your phone.

And while some radiator fans are driven by the drive belt, others have an electric motor.

And, of course, your electrical system is what powers your headlights, turn signals, taillights, and brake lights.

Turn on your lights and tap your brakes, Lena.

Okay.

Looks like it's the upper light that's out.

Easy enough to replace, if it's just the bulb and not a short in the wiring.

How do you know if it's a wiring problem and not just a dead bulb?

The new bulb won't work.

The taillight covers are held on by bolts. You can access these bolts by opening your trunk or hatchback.

Sometimes they're right there, and sometimes they're hidden behind a panel.

(You might be lucky; some cars have an access hatch behind the taillight that will allow you to change the bulb without removing the bolts!)

On a pickup truck, you'll usually see the bolts when you open the tailgate.

Remove the bolts and then pull free the bulb housing, which is the big colored plastic pieces visible on the back of the vehicle.

Now comes the easy part... getting to the bulb!

Yours has two: an upper and a lower light on either side of the turn signal blinker.

Find the bulb by following the wire.

The wire usually ends at a knob. Twist the knob counter-clockwise...

And voilà! You've got your bulb.

Don't touch the glass part of the new bulb, or the oil from your skin will burn it out more quickly.

Swap it out for the old one and retrace your steps to put everything back how it was when you started.

What about headlights? Is it the same type of thing?

Sometimes, but the newer the car, the more likely that accessing the headlights will be tricky.

But we spent **less** than what we've saved up.

Which is good, because it's going to cost a real chunk to get it up and running.

We **were** going to wait to tell you guys until we had a chance to do some more work on it.

Esther's just embarrassed because it's in real rough shape right now.

Me, I can't wait to show you guys!

If Esther doesn't mind us seeing it before it's up to snuff, you won't **have** to. We could finish out the day looking at your new vehicle.

Okay.

Just so long as you know...

"...it's got a **long** way to go."

It's missing a door!

And a hood, **and** an alternator, **and** some seats, **and** tires, **and** a drive belt, **and** a real fuel tank, **and** brakes, **and** a windshield...

Like I said, it's got a long way to go.

It looks pretty banged up. Was it in an accident?

I wouldn't call it an **accident**.

Our neighbor got it running just enough to enter it in a demolition derby a couple of months back.

What's a demolition derby?

It's like bumper cars, only with **real** cars. Last one that can still move is the winner.

Sounds dangerous.

Our neighbor once jumped off the roof into a plastic wading pool and broke both of his ankles.

"Dangerous" doesn't usually factor into his decision-making.

So did he win?

Not even close. Car died and he couldn't restart it.

*The **alternator** uses the running engine to recharge the battery (see page 88)!

"...we'll spend our last meeting on your new car!"

If you're replacing an alternator, the first thing you'd **usually** do is disconnect the battery, for safety.

"Usually" because the twins took the battery out already?

Yep.

So we go straight for the alternator itself.

We'll use a socket wrench to loosen the bolts that connect the alternator to the engine.

Any time you remove bolts, nuts, washers, **anything**, put them all in a spot where you won't lose them or knock them over.*

The serpentine belt is already loose, or we'd loosen it.

The belt runs across the alternator pulley, so you wouldn't be able to remove the alternator if the belt weren't slack!

Alternators are connected to the car's electrical system via a wire or wires.

Once the bolts are removed, you can carefully pull the alternator out of its dock to reach and disconnect them.

Then you just **repeat** all of those steps **in reverse** with the new alternator:

Connect the wires, slide the new alternator into place, tighten the bolts, and tighten the belt.

On it!

*You can get a magnetic tray at most auto part stores that's perfect for this job!

And when she's done, I've got the battery. It was charged a couple weeks back, but it's been sitting, so it may need a jump to get it going.

It's not drained, so I figure that the alternator can recharge it if we get it running.

Speaking of batteries, I worked on mine this week.

Worked on it, how?

I noticed it had that blue sandy buildup on the terminals.

So I mixed up a cleaning solution* and cleaned it.

*Page 25!

Were you, like, showing your engine off or something?

Nope.

I was checking my oil and just saw the gunk and figured I'd clean it away.

Abner! I'm so proud of you.

You are? How come?

Checking your oil? Cleaning your battery connections?

Thus far, your only concern for your car has been for its **appearance**.

Well, yeah...

...but that was back when its appearance wasn't **perfect**.

That's right! And if you can't remember, there's an easy way to tell.

Look for a line that connects one of the terminal connectors to the vehicle's body. That's how the circuit is grounded, and that's the grounded cable, the one that should be the first off and the last on.

These terminals are often made of lead, so be sure to wash your hands **really** well after handling them.

You should wash your hands after doing **any** car work, but lead especially can do real damage to those brains of yours, so you don't want to accidentally touch your lunch or something without getting any traces off your skin.

The positive cable is on. Now I can put on the negative cable.

You just shimmy the loose connectors down onto the terminals, and then use the connector's nut and bolt to tighten it in place.

Think we should try to start it?

We might as well try.

Abner, do you have a set of jumper cables in your car?

'Fraid not, Ms. G.

Now **that** is a tool worth keeping in your trunk!

You never know when your car might need a jump to get it home or to a repair shop, and even if you never need it for **yourself**, you'll encounter plenty of **other** people who will.

You may not be in a position to help everyone you encounter, but if you have your own set of jumper cables, you'll at least have the option if you **are** in such a position.

Like a superhero for parking lots!

Okay, first thing's first. Make sure that both cars are off and that they're safely in park.

Or up on cinder blocks.

Does **anyone** here have jumper cables?

I got some, Ms. Gritt.

...**and** applying the clamp directly to the battery terminal **could** produce an otherwise harmless **spark**.

The spark could ignite that escaping hydrogen...

...creating a violent, acid-spewing **explosion**!

Oh no! Dead again!

This is the second time you've mentioned violent, acid-spewing explosions.

Are they, like, **common**?

Oh, good heavens, no!

But mentioning them certainly gets your attention!

No, we clamp the final cable to the car's body for a steadier current, not to prevent violent, acid-spewing explosions.

A cracked or damaged battery is the **real** cause of that kind of danger, so remember to never use a dropped battery or one that is obviously damaged.

Now, the cars are off, but it's very important to make sure that none of the electrical systems are in use.

Headlights

Radio or sound system

Seat warmers

Cabin lights

GPS

Defroster (unless your manual says to have it running during battery jumps)

Windshield wipers

Air conditioner

And make sure to unplug your phone charger!

Right! The jolt from the battery jump can fry a phone's circuits.

5 Turn on the car with the working battery and let it idle for five or ten minutes.

On it!

VROOM

I'm really going to miss working with you guys.

Hey, there's no reason you can't pick Car Club up again after break.

Yeah, there is. Track starts up in January and she's the coach.

My schedule only gives me a window of a few weeks to do Car Club, but I'm sure grateful for those few weeks.

We certainly haven't covered everything, or even a small fraction of everything...

...but what we have covered should give you enough of a foundation to further explore the workings and maintenance of your vehicles.

And even if you don't try to move beyond what we covered, you've still gotten the basic know-how that you need to safely drive and maintain your car.

Well, Abner's car has been giving the twins' car juice long enough to give it a try. See if it'll start.

All right. Take two.

RRRRRRVWWRM

Oh, man. It works! It really works!

Yeah. Yeah, it does!

Great! Now we disconnect the jumper cables, reversing the order of how we attached them.

Making sure the clamps don't touch each other, and taking off the one attached to the unpainted metal first.

Feel that shaking? That's really rough for an idling engine.

Started kind of jumpy, too.

You know what we need to replace...

...the spark plugs.

All right, guys. I've got to go. Thanks again for being a part of Car Club, and I'll see you in school after break!

Even though Car Club is over, we have a few pages left in the book.

So let's talk about some of the stuff that we didn't cover.

ACCELERATION

Near the floor under the steering wheel, you've got at least a couple of pedals.

On the left* is the **brake pedal**. We talked about brakes on page 17.

But on the right is the **acceleration pedal**, also called the **gas pedal** or the **accelerator**.

Brake

Gas

The gas pedal doesn't actually control the **gas**. What it does control is the **throttle valve**.

When you press the gas pedal, it makes the throttle valve open. The harder you press the pedal, the wider the valve opens.

Remember how your engine's pistons are put into motion by lots of tiny explosions (page 15)? Well, explosions are just sudden bursts of energy, in this case fire.

Fire needs two things to burn: **air** and **fuel**.

The throttle valve is the opening through which you give the engine air. Push the pedal down, and air rushes in to make that burn possible.

IDLE ENGINE	ACCELERATING	FULL THROTTLE
Closed valve (no air to burn).	Letting in air allows the fuel to burn, moving the car.	Fully open, the car will burn as much fuel as it can.

*If you've got a manual transmission, the brake pedal will be in the middle, and on the left, you'll have the clutch pedal.

Clutch Brake Gas

(Look back on page 20 for a refresher on how the transmission works.)

The clutch pedal discontinues power to the transmission gears.

When it is pressed, the gears can be switched using a stick shift.

Because no power flows through the gears when the clutch is in, pressing the gas pedal won't result in acceleration until the clutch is released.

If your car was made in the last fifty years or so, it has electronic sensors or a computer that measures how much air you're letting in, and it increases the rate that the fuel (gasoline or diesel) flows in to match.

So fuel and air are the ingredients necessary for those little explosions to happen, but what sets them off? What's the match that lights that fire?

SPARK PLUGS

Spark plugs ignite the mixture of fuel and air as part of a **four-stroke** engine cycle. Here's how:

Intake valve

Fuel particles

Spark plug

Cylinder

Exhaust valve

Piston

Crank-shaft

The **crankshaft** spins to power the transmission, the car's belts, and to keep the multiple pistons pumping.

1 First is the **intake** stroke.

The piston goes down, and in doing so, pulls a mixture of air and fuel through an open valve into the cylinder.

2 Second is the **compression** stroke.

The intake valve closes as the piston goes up, compressing the fuel and air mixture into a tight, volatile, ready-to-explode mixture.

3 Third is the **combustion** stroke.

The **spark plug** creates a spark, igniting the tightly compressed fuel mixture and creating an explosion that drives the cylinder down with incredible force. It is this stroke that forces the crankshaft to turn, allowing the cycle to continue.

4 Fourth is the **exhaust** stroke.

As the exhaust valve opens, the piston goes up again, pushing the burnt air/fuel mix out into the exhaust system.

Then the cycle **repeats**!

Your car or truck or SUV is going to hit a lot of bumps when it's out on the road. Or off the road!

But don't worry, your vehicle was designed to take on these bumps using its **suspension** system.

SUSPENSION

When your wheel hits a bump, it goes over it. The wheel is attached to something that will allow it to go up without raising the vehicle.

This "something" might be a coiled spring...

...or a swinging arm...

...or a leaf spring like on Lena's truck (page 33)...

...or other cushioners that serve the same purpose.

But what keeps these cushioners from continuing to bounce after absorbing the impact?

SHOCK ABSORBERS!

Shock absorbers, or **shocks**, are hydraulic tubes filled with oil, located next to or even inside the cushioners.

Inside, there are tiny holes through which the oil flows, and the faster the piston (a rod inside the tube) moves, the slower the oil flows. This helps the shock absorber absorb the different bumps evenly, being more rigid or more loose as the situation demands.

Shocks last a long time, but if your ride is bouncier than you'd like, you might need to replace them.

Push down on your vehicle at each corner. If it bounces up and down after you let go, you probably need new shocks.

While cautious driving and alertness to your surroundings are the best ways to keep yourself and your passengers safe...

...your car has some built-in safety functions that protect you in the event of an accident.

SEAT BELTS & AIRBAGS

When your vehicle is traveling, you're traveling at the same speed. If it collides with something, it stops suddenly... but **you don't**.

Your **seat belt** keeps you from crashing into the dashboard, the steering wheel, or the windshield, all of which could cause serious injury or death.

The seat belt applies the force needed to stop your momentum, spreading that force over a wide, sturdy part of your body to minimize that force.

Seat belt webbing is strong but flexible (at least more flexible than your windshield!),

Usually you can lean forward with your seat belt buckled, thanks to a spooling mechanism called the **retractor**.

But when the car rapidly decelerates or when the belt is jerked, that spool locks in place, keeping you tight (and safe) against your seat.

Even with seat belts, an impact can be very damaging. Another way car manufacturers try to lessen that danger is with the use of **airbags**.

Newer cars are fitted with an impact sensor. If your car hits something, the airbags are deployed to help cushion you.

Airbags have to inflate in the blink of an eye. Fuel inside the inflator is ignited, producing gas to inflate the bag.

The inflated bag puffs up to its full size in time to cushion the impact created by the collision.

The gas almost immediately begins to escape through tiny holes so that you can get out of the car.

An airbag can be a lifesaver, but if you're not wearing your seat belt properly (with its shoulder strap) then an airbag can cause serious injury!

We talked about how your car's heater works on page 15.

But when it's hot out, you don't need a heater.

Luckily, your car has an **air conditioner** for when the temperature outside is making the vehicle's inside uncomfortable.

AIR CONDITIONER

Your car's air-conditioning system is filled with a fluid called **refrigerant**. It changes back and forth from liquid to gas depending on both its temperature and how much pressure it's under.

1
As a **gas** under **low pressure**, the refrigerant goes into the **compressor** where it is compressed into a high-pressure gas.

4
The **liquid** refrigerant, now at **low pressure**, flows through the **evaporator**. Inside it boils into a low-pressure gas again, pulling the heat away from its coils and chilling them with its condensation.

2
That **high-pressure gas** enters the **condenser**, which works like the radiator,* letting the air from outside cool the refrigerant into a liquid under high pressure.

The coldness of the evaporator is blown into the vehicle's cabin through vents, cooling the air inside the car.

The **high-pressure liquid** flows through an **expansion valve**, which allows it to expand and lose its pressure.
3

*See how radiators work on page 15!

Well, that's it! I think we've covered all the big stuff, right?

Are you kidding? We haven't talked about the most important thing of all!

SOUND SYSTEMS

Your sound system starts with the head unit. This is the control center of your sound system and is found on your dashboard, usually in the center between the driver and passenger seats.

MUSIC AND STUFF

From here, you can control what plays, the source of the sounds,* and the sound settings. In newer systems you can link your head unit to your phone for hands-free talking.

There are as many as three components in most sound systems.

Speakers reproduce sound. Your vehicle probably came with speakers, but you can change them out for fancier ones if you want to.

Subwoofers help to boost the bass (the lower register) of the sound being sent to the speakers. These usually have to be added to a sound system.

Amplifiers boost the power of the electrical signal from the source to the speakers to make it louder. It also translates the signal to make it more clear.

AM Radio
AM comes from a continuous signal broadcast through the air via radio waves. The degree to which that signal is amplified determines the sound.

FM Radio
FM also comes from a continuous radio signal, but its sounds are determined by slight deviations in the frequency at which the signal is broadcast.

Satellite Radio
Satellite subscription services project signals up into outer space where they are transmitted back to earth by a satellite. Cars with satellite antennae can receive these signals.

Your Own Music
You may have music on your phone, on an MP3 player, on a disc, or on a cassette tape. Your head unit may have a way to play music from these formats.

Hi, I'm Chris, and I'm the fella who wrote and drew this book.

When I was younger, I didn't know **anything** about cars, except how to drive them too fast and how to accidentally back into mailboxes.

Uh-oh.

I figured that car engines were **too complicated** to figure out. Better leave them to the experts!

But one day, when I was an adult, my car wouldn't start.

I mentioned this to a neighbor, just griping...

YOU COULD DO IT YOURSELF

Turns out that the only thing I needed to start fixing my own car was the confidence that I could. Someone telling me that I could* gave me that confidence!

By reading an online tutorial and watching a YouTube video...

great resources for car maintenance...

I changed the starter myself. My first car repair!

*And guess what? I'm telling you that **you** can, **too**!

Now I do a lot of my own repairs, and each time I learn a little more about my vehicle, how it works, and how I can help it to work **better**.

Oh no! We're supposed to be guests at a comic convention, and now we're going to be **late**!

Not if **I** have anything to say about it!

Homemade bumper with a winch plate (no winch, though)

There are tons of good books about cars and car maintenance out there, but here are a few that I've found especially useful.

THIS IS A 1995 EDITION. SEE INFO ON 1990s REVISIONS IN FRONT COVER

Auto Mechanics Fundamentals
Martin W. Stockel / Martin T. Stockel

Auto Mechanics Fundamentals
by Martin W. Stockel and Martin T. Stockel

This book explains how engines work by presenting each component as the solution to a problem. It makes everything seem very practical and helps you to understand why the parts exist and what they do. This is my very top pick if you want to understand, well, the fundamentals of auto mechanics.

Saturday Mechanic and Complete Car Care Manual
from *Popular Mechanics*

These are handy books for understanding and fixing all sorts of problems. They've got clear illustrations and instructions and are great to have on hand.

Haynes Automotive Repair Manuals
from Haynes Publishing

The writers and illustrators of the manuals published by Haynes completely disassemble the cars that are the subject of their manuals and, in putting them back together, create a far more detailed and comprehensive guide to your specific vehicle than your owner's manual.

JEEP CHEROKEE
1984 thru 1999
Cherokee □ Wagoneer □ Comanche
Automotive Repair Manual

I keep **my** Haynes Manual in my car. You never know when you might be somewhere with no phone service, but you can reference a book **anywhere**!

Also, the internet is a great resource for car tips, process tutorials, videos, and tips from mechanics and manufacturers alike!

Happy fixing!

GET TO KNOW YOUR UNIVERSE!

SCIENCE COMICS

"An excellent addition to school and classroom libraries."
—School Library Journal

...And more books coming soon!